RESCUE DOGS ON 9/11

BY AMY C. REA

childsworld.com

Published by The Child's World®
800-599-READ • www.childsworld.com

Photography Credits

Photographs ©: Andrea Booher/FEMA/AP Images, cover, 1; Shutterstock Images, 5, 9; D. Fahleson/Houston Chronicle/AP Images, 6; Spc. Andrea K. Serhan/CAISE/DVIDS, 10 (cadaver dog); Lance Cpl. Victoria Ross/US Marine Corps/DVIDS, 10 (avalanche dog); Sgt. John Crosby/DVIDS, 10 (water dog); Sgt. 1st Class Aaron Tinsley/Indiana National Guard/DVIDS, 10 (urban disaster dog); Brad Rhen/Pennsylvania National Guard/DVIDS, 10 (trailing dog); Karen Warren/Houston Chronicle/AP Images, 11; Joseph Sohm/Shutterstock Images, 12; Eve Photography/Shutterstock Images, 14; Stephen Chernin/AP Images, 16; Master Sgt. Mark Olsen/US Air National Guard/DVIDS, 18; George Best/Getty Images News/Getty Images, 19; David McNew/Getty Images News/Getty Images, 20; Tech. Sgt. Parker Gyokeres/US Air Force/DVIDS, 21; Journalist 1st Class Preston Keres/US Navy, 22; Guillermo Ossa/Shutterstock Images, 25; Jake Schoellkopf/AP Images, 26; Staff Sgt. Taylor Harrison/US Air Force/DVIDS, 28

ISBN Information
9781503889125 (Reinforced Library Binding)
9781503890886 (Portable Document Format)
9781503892125 (Online Multi-user eBook)
9781503893368 (Electronic Publication)

LCCN 2023950402

Printed in the United States of America

ABOUT THE AUTHOR

Amy C. Rea grew up in northern Minnesota and now lives in a Minneapolis suburb with her family. She writes frequently about traveling around Minnesota and loves spending time with her family and her silly dog.

CONTENTS

FAST FACTS

- On September 11, 2001, **terrorists** took over four airplanes. They crashed the planes into the World Trade Center in New York City and the Pentagon near Washington, DC. A fourth plane crashed in a field near Shanksville, Pennsylvania, after its passengers fought the terrorists.
- There are many dogs trained to do search and rescue. The Federal Emergency Management Agency (FEMA) has more than 300 canine search teams.
- Bretagne was the last living 9/11 search dog. She died in 2016.
- Tikva was a keeshond sent to be a comfort dog for workers at the World Trade Center.
- A dog named Trakr helped locate the last survivor found at the World Trade Center. The woman had been trapped for 27 hours after the attacks.
- Riley was a live-search dog who was brought in to find survivors.
- Sage was a dog working at the Pentagon. She found the body of one of the terrorists in the rubble.
- Some of the dogs won awards for their rescue work, including the work they did after the 9/11 attacks.

Some of the earliest rescue dogs were trained near the Great Saint Bernard Pass in Europe. In the 1700s, monks at a monastery near this dangerous pass began using Saint Bernard dogs to rescue lost travelers.

CHAPTER ONE

BRETAGNE AND DENISE

It was September 11, 2001. Denise Corliss lived in Texas with her two-year-old golden retriever, Bretagne. Bretagne's name is pronounced like *Brittany*. This is the English name of the French region the dog was named after. Corliss had trained Bretagne as a search and rescue (SAR) dog.

Denise Corliss and Bretagne were photographed in Texas on the one-year anniversary of 9/11.

Bretagne was trained to help find people trapped after **disasters**. Her training was complete. But she had not yet been put to work.

Then two planes hit the Twin Towers of the World Trade Center in New York City. Within a few days, Corliss and Bretagne were assigned to search for people at the World Trade Center site. They arrived in New York and were taken to the piles of **debris**. It was Bretagne's first job as a SAR dog.

Bretagne was ready. Her nose twitched, sensing all the different smells around the site. She was trained to use her sense of smell to find where people might be buried under the rubble. She crawled around and climbed over piles of broken pieces of the World Trade Center, always sniffing. Corliss thought they would be searching for survivors. But it quickly became clear that they would only find remains.

The work was hard. Bretagne searched 12 hours a day for 10 days. But she did not find a live person. Very few people had survived the collapse of the Twin Towers. Like people, dogs can become unhappy. It can be discouraging for a dog and its handler to look for survivors and not find any. But Bretagne began serving a different kind of role. There were many **first responders** helping with the search. They were unhappy, too.

Some of them began coming over to see Bretagne. She was a friendly dog. The first responders would pet her and watch her tail wag. They would talk to Corliss about the work they were doing. Some of them were looking for friends and family members in the rubble. Taking a break to pet Bretagne and talk to Corliss made them feel better. They could continue with the hard work. One of Corliss's coworkers said, "It was really heartwarming to see these big, rough firefighters and rescue people sit down next to Bretagne. Bretagne would put her head in their laps, and you'd see the tension come off their faces. For a few minutes, you could just see it: This is comfort."

September 11 was Bretagne's first job, and it was a hard one. In later years, she helped search disaster areas after Hurricane Katrina, Hurricane Rita, and Hurricane Ivan. Bretagne **retired** from search and rescue when she was nine years old. But she continued to make public appearances. She also helped students who were learning how to read. In 2014, Bretagne and Corliss were invited to visit the 9/11 Memorial in New York City. It was the first time they had been back since 2001. Bretagne was also honored at the Hero Dog Awards in 2014. She was invited back to New York for her 16th birthday in 2015. She stayed in a fancy hotel, got a special hamburger, and received lots of toys and treats.

The 9/11 Memorial and Museum displays many objects to teach the public about the September 11 attacks, including this steel beam recovered from the World Trade Center. ►

PAPD
37
L101
L132
MJB
1

TYPES OF SAR DOGS

There are many different types of SAR dogs. Each dog is trained for a special purpose.

AIR-SCENTING DOGS

Air-scenting dogs search for human scent in the air. These dogs look for any people in a certain area.

Cadaver Dogs look for human remains.

Avalanche and Wilderness Dogs help find people buried under snow or lost in the wilderness.

Water Dogs are specially trained to find people in or under the water

Urban Disaster Dogs help find people in the rubble of collapsed buildings.

TRAILING DOGS

Trailing dogs follow the trail of a specific human's scent on the ground. They need a piece of clothing with the scent to get started.

Denise Corliss accompanied Bretagne to the dog's final veterinary appointment.

By 2016, Bretagne's health was failing. Corliss took her to the veterinarian for the last time. They were met by several first responders who saluted as Bretagne slowly walked in. When Corliss brought out Bretagne's body draped in an American flag, the first responders saluted again.

ESSEX COUNTY SALUTES
THE SEARCH & RESCUE DOGS OF 9/11/2001
Histories are more full of examples of the fidelity of dogs than of friends.
~Alexander Pope, English Poet
More than 350 search and rescue dogs were called into action on September 11, 2001.
They scrambled over the smoldering debris of the Twin Towers, using all their senses
to locate survivors ~ to no avail. From Daschunds to Golden Retrievers, dogs and their owners,
all well-trained for the mission, were stunned by their inability to find a living soul.
They did their best at the Pentagon site, as well. As the reality of the situation became starkly evident,
depression reached the first responders, the owners and their animals, and soon,
the dogs began to play another role ~ that of comforter. They snuggled close to workers
taking a moment of respite from their grueling labors, rested a head upon a knee, the men and women
drawing solace from the warm touch of the animal ~ and the dog rewarded with strokes and soft words.
Search and rescue dogs have served during traumatic events throughout the world, from
Oklahoma City to Haiti, reminding us, over and over, of the unbreakable bonds we share.
Dedicated August 17, 2016
Joseph N. DiVincenzo, Jr.
Essex County Executive
and the
Board of Chosen Freeholders
~ Putting Essex County First ~
COUNTY OF ESSEX
NEW JERSEY
COUNTY OF ESSEX
NEW JERSEY

CHAPTER TWO

TIKVA AND CINDY

Cindy Ehlers owned a keeshond named Tikva, which means "hope" in Hebrew. Tikva was only one year old on September 11, 2001. After the attacks, Ehlers brought Tikva to the World Trade Center site. It was one of the first times Tikva had worked as a crisis response dog. Crisis response dogs are sometimes called comfort dogs.

Unlike dogs that were trained to search for people, Tikva had a different purpose. Her job was to help the human workers by comforting them and giving them much-needed breaks and affection. Crisis response dogs are taken to all kinds of places where people are stressed and unhappy. Not all therapy dogs can become crisis response dogs. Crisis response dogs must remain calm and unafraid, even if the humans around them are stressed or upset. They cannot let the surroundings upset them.

A memorial in New Jersey honors the working dogs of 9/11.

Keeshonden are friendly, fluffy, medium-sized dogs.

Many therapy dogs sent to the World Trade Center were not able to finish the work. But Tikva was able to. She was calm and cute and helped distract the responders from the disaster around them. Tikva also stood out because of her breed. Many of the other dogs working at the World Trade Center were border collies, golden retrievers, and Labrador retrievers. A keeshond was a less common dog breed.

One person Tikva helped was an emergency medical technician (EMT). EMTs provide emergency medical care to people who are ill or injured but are not at a doctor's office or hospital. The EMT said Tikva changed his life. Seeing her was the only time he could smile during those hard days.

Ehlers said, "A firefighter called up . . . after we left and said, 'Where are those comfort dogs? They're the only thing that helps me get through the day.'" Tikva seemed to know what people needed. She would rub her face into someone's hand or tap her nose against a human's face. If she sat in someone's lap, she cuddled up and tucked her face into the crook of the person's arm.

After 9/11, Tikva went to other places to help people who needed comfort, including the site of Hurricane Katrina. Later, she worked with the American Red Cross, which is a worldwide disaster response group. She would go with Red Cross workers to visit hospital patients and victims of house fires. "There was something about them," Ehlers said. "She could tell that they were going through something difficult."

Tikva lived until 2014. Her owner continued to train crisis response dogs. She founded Hope Animal-Assisted Crisis Response, which helps find crisis response dogs to send where they are needed to comfort people.

REGIONAL
POLICE
POLICE

CHAPTER THREE

TRAKR AND JAMES

On the morning of September 11, 2001, a woman named Genelle Guzman-McMillan was on the 64th floor of the North Tower when the first plane hit. She tried to escape by going down the stairs. But as she reached the 13th floor, the building collapsed around her. She felt the walls cave in. Everything around her was dark, and she could hear rumbling noises. Her head was trapped by a concrete pillar. But her face was in an area where there was air, so she could breathe.

James Symington was a Canadian police officer. He worked with Trakr, a German shepherd trained as a police dog. Trakr had previously helped find more than $1 million in stolen goods. He also helped find missing people. Trakr had been retired from police work. But when Symington heard what happened in New York, he felt that Trakr might be able to help.

James Symington and Trakr came from Canada to help with search and rescue after the September 11 attacks.

A SAR dog rests near the World Trade Center site on September 14, 2001.

Symington took Trakr and drove more than 14 hours from his home in Canada. Together, they began searching around the debris. Trakr was sniffing for signs of life.

Early in the morning of September 12, Trakr found something. He froze and stiffened his tail as he was trained to do. That was a sign to Symington that Trakr might have found a survivor. Trakr's signals and excitement alerted other rescue workers that they should dig in that area. One rescuer in the area saw a shiny piece of fabric. That helped lead them to Guzman-McMillan. While Trakr had not found her exact spot, it was close enough.

Apollo was another 9/11 SAR dog. He and his handler, Officer Peter Davis, were the first SAR dog team on the scene to look for survivors.

DAVIS
23413
CANINE

In 2009, Symington won a contest to have Trakr cloned. Cloning an animal means taking its DNA and creating a copy. Five clones of Trakr (pictured) were born later that year.

Rescuers pulled Guzman-McMillan from the rubble. She was the final survivor found. She later said, "It's so awesome that the dogs could have this kind of sense, to find people buried under the rubble. . . . That was the most joyful moment."

SAR operations are tiring for dogs and handlers alike.

Excited by the success, Symington and Trakr continued searching for another day. But the two long days of work were hard on Trakr. On the second day, he collapsed from exhaustion, smoke **inhalation**, and burns. He was treated for his injuries and survived. Symington and Trakr returned to Canada, but it was Trakr's final search duty. In 2005, Trakr and Symington were awarded the Extraordinary Service to Humanity Award by Jane Goodall. Goodall is a scientist who has studied animal behavior and promotes wildlife education and **conservation**. Rick Cushman worked with Trakr and Symington during the search effort. He said, "That dog was a hero, all right."

CHAPTER FOUR

RILEY AND CHRIS

Riley was a four-year-old golden retriever living with his owner, Chris Selfridge, in Pennsylvania. Riley had worked as a SAR dog during two hurricanes. But being called to the World Trade Center after the September 11 attacks was his biggest job yet. Riley was brought in to help find survivors in the rubble. But after many hours, he had not found any. Riley did find some human remains, including the bodies of several firefighters. Riley was trained to find living people, not bodies. But Selfridge said Riley and other dogs seemed to adjust to the change. Instead of barking like he was trained to do when finding a survivor, Riley would paw at the ground. "I think the dogs had a sense [that] they needed to do something different," Selfridge said. "They were trying to tell us, 'Hey, there's something going on here. It's not really my job, but maybe you need to look here a little more.'"

SAR teams used ropes and a basket to transport heavy equipment. Riley's handler used the system to send him quickly and safely across a long distance. This photo of Riley became one of the most famous of 9/11 rescue dogs.

Not finding survivors was difficult for Riley and the other rescue dogs. Some handlers staged rescues so the dogs would feel successful. Someone would pretend to be a survivor buried in the rubble. Finding the person would lift the dog's spirits. The experience was discouraging for first responders, too. But the rescue dogs lifted their spirits. Selfridge said, "I tried my best to tell Riley he was doing his job. He had no way to know that when firefighters and police officers came over to hug him, and for a split second you can see them crack a smile—that Riley was succeeding at doing an altogether different job. He provided comfort."

Riley lived to be 13 years old. He died in 2010 from cancer. Some veterinarians and SAR dog owners wondered if dogs like Riley were sickened by their work at the World Trade Center. In the days after the attacks, the air was full of **pollution**. Dogs and humans inhaled it while they worked.

SAR dogs must be obedient. They must also be smart. For example, if a handler commands a dog to leave an area but the dog has found someone, the dog should not obey.

CHAPTER FIVE

SAGE AND DIANE

Sage was a two-year-old border collie who lived with her owner, Diane Whetsel, in New Mexico. Whetsel trained Sage to be a rescue dog. When Sage was 18 months old, she became a **certified** Federal Emergency Management Agency (FEMA) SAR dog. FEMA is a government organization that sends people to help in areas affected by disasters. FEMA has more than 300 canine search teams. Sage had FEMA's highest certification. This meant she was considered one of the best of the best.

The World Trade Center was the biggest target on September 11, 2001. But terrorists also attacked the Pentagon near Washington, DC. This building is the headquarters of the US military. Part of the building had collapsed. Whetsel and Sage were sent to help the rescue efforts at the Pentagon.

Sage and Diane Whetsel (holding leash) met future New Mexico Governor Bill Richardson (left) in 2002.

SAR dogs and their handlers often develop a close bond.

With her powerful nose, Sage found the body of the terrorist who flew the plane into the building. People began calling her the Wonder Dog.

That was Sage's first big assignment. She continued to work on many others. She searched for survivors of Hurricanes Katrina and Rita. In 2007 and 2008, she went to war zones in Iraq. She searched for the bodies of soldiers who had died. Sage also became a source of comfort. "Sage turned out to be the warm fur for soldiers to cry into, or just a playmate," Whetsel said. "She would always bring a smile to the soldiers' faces."

In 2009, Sage received the Award for Canine Excellence in the Search and Rescue category from the American Kennel Club. Two years later, the American Humane Association named her a Hero Dog. Sage died in 2012 after battling cancer. Sage had been involved in studies about the effects of pollution on 9/11 SAR dogs. Whetsel donated Sage's body for research. "Sage's life of service has been all-encompassing, with her service to the country in so many places," Whetsel said. "But this might be her biggest contribution, paying it forward even in her death." Whetsel also created the Sage Foundation. This group helps working dogs who have been injured in the line of duty.

THINK ABOUT IT

- Is it a good idea to use dogs for search and rescue or for comforting humans? Why or why not?
- Many 9/11 SAR dogs also ended up providing comfort. Why do you think dogs might do a better job at providing comfort than other people?
- Why would it be hard for a trained SAR dog to not find any survivors? Can you imagine how that dog might feel?

GLOSSARY

certified (SIR-tih-fyed): Someone who is certified has passed tests and meets special qualifications. Sage was a FEMA-certified SAR dog.

conservation (kon-sir-VAY-shun): Conservation happens when something is protected from harm or loss. Dr. Jane Goodall works for wildlife conservation.

debris (duh-BREE): Debris is made up of pieces of things that have been destroyed or broken down. SAR dogs searched for survivors in the debris after the Twin Towers collapsed.

disasters (dih-ZASS-ters): Disasters are events that cause large amounts of damage. SAR dogs are used to help find people after disasters.

first responders (FURST rih-SPAWN-durs): First responders are people who arrive quickly at the scene of a disaster, such as police or firefighters. Many SAR dogs also ended up giving comfort to first responders.

inhalation (in-huh-LAY-shun): Inhalation is material that has been inhaled, or breathed in. Smoke inhalation can be very dangerous for the lungs.

pollution (puh-LOO-shun): Pollution includes materials that can make the air hard to breathe or water dangerous to drink. The pollution after 9/11 made the air dangerous to breathe.

retired (rih-TIRED): When someone is retired, she no longer works at a job. Bretagne retired from SAR work.

terrorists (TAYR-ur-ists): Terrorists are people who commit violent acts to make people feel fear or terror. Sage found the body of one of the terrorists at the site of the Pentagon attacks.

SELECTED BIBLIOGRAPHY

9/11 Memorial Staff. "Four-Legged 9/11 Heroes." *9/11 Memorial*, n.d., www.911memorial.org. Accessed 13 Dec. 2023.

Domonoske, Camila. "Last Known Sept. 11 Search Dog, Bretagne, Dies at 16." *NPR*, 7 Jun. 2016, www.npr.org. Accessed 13 Dec. 2023.

Mietus, Dana. "9/11 Dogs You've Probably Never Heard Of." *American Kennel Club*, 19 Sept. 2023, www.akc.org. Accessed 13 Dec. 2023.

FIND OUT MORE

BOOKS

Buckley, James, Jr. *Canine Hero*. Minneapolis, MN: Bearport, 2022.

Couch, Christina, and Cara Giaimo. *Detector Dogs, Dynamite Dolphins, and More Animals with Super Sensory Powers*. Somerville, MA: MIT Kids Press, 2022.

Hamen, Susan E. *Survivors on 9/11*. Parker, CO: The Child's World, 2025.

WEBSITES

Visit our website for links about rescue dogs:
childsworld.com/links

Note to Parents, Caregivers, Teachers, and Librarians: We routinely verify our web links to make sure they are safe and active sites. So encourage your readers to check them out!

INDEX